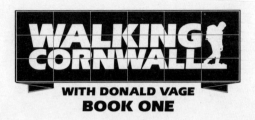

WITH DONALD VAGE
BOOK ONE

**TEN CORNISH COUNTRYSIDE
& COASTAL WALKS
WITH MAPS & PHOTOGRAPHS**

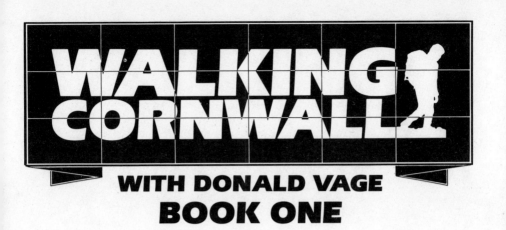

WALKING CORNWALL

WITH DONALD VAGE
BOOK ONE

TEN CORNISH COUNTRYSIDE
& COASTAL WALKS
WITH MAPS & PHOTOGRAPHS

First published in 1987 by Devon Books
ISBN 0 86114 809 6

Design, Typesetting by Richards Typesetting & Design Ltd. Exeter.
Printed by A. Wheaton & Co. Ltd. Exeter.

BOOK ONE
CONTENTS

FOREWORD

"THE reflections on a day well spent furnish us with joys more pleasing than ten thousand triumphs."

THOMAS À KEMPIS.

How lucky I have been to be born in my beloved Cornwall and to be fit enough to enjoy its beauty by walking in quiet and peaceful byways with my wife (41 happy years) and little dog 'Tessa' — and 'Minnie' before her.

These ten walks first appeared in monthly editions of *Cornish Life* magazine. They are suggested in a general way rather than by explicit instruction, as I would like you to vary them a little to suit your own inclination or investigate what is 'round the corner'. I use the 1: 50,000 Ordnance Survey series of maps (about 1 ¼ inches to the mile), but you may wish to use the larger scale 1: 25,000 maps which even show field boundaries. We have provided rough maps of each walk to give general directional help.

With very few exceptions the walks are designed to be 'circular' and none are too difficult for the ordinary fit person in their 'sixties', as we are.

Most people use their car to find the starting point of a walk, returning to it at journey's end, but I have tried to indicate places where family groups can meet (perhaps the halfway point) so that small grandchildren and Great Aunt Agnes can still feel part of the family 'day out' at picnic time.

If advice were needed, I should first of all suggest good-quality comfortable waterproof boots, a rucksack with lightweight waterproof clothing, food (and water for the dog), and I always carry an emergency miniature torch, multi-bladed knife and compass, together with a packet of Elastoplast.

For those with a particular interest in bird-watching or ship recognition, I suggest carrying in the rucksack lightweight miniature prismatic binoculars with a 6 x magnification. My camera hardly ever leaves me, and it is always 'at the ready' for the unexpected shot.

I have not forgotten the very elderly or disabled and have suggested many points where they could enjoy wonderful scenery and perhaps a short level walk on even ground.

I have no specialist knowledge in geology, biology or any other related subject, so you can, I hope, enjoy these walks through the eyes of an 'interested Cornishman'.

DONALD VAGE, 1987.

WALK ONE

Deep winding lanes of wild flowers, peaceful tidal creeks and three delightful villages.

MANACCAN TO ST ANTHONY-IN-MENEAGE AND HELFORD

OS Map (1: 50,000) 204. Length: Approximately six miles.

MANACCAN is not the easiest village to find (it lies at the head of a creek just south of the Helford River), but driving slowly through the surrounding deeply incised lanes bordered with colourful valerian and campion is all part of this glorious excursion.

Arriving at the centre of the village we begin our walk by visiting the fine old church, dedicated to St Manacca, one of two Cornish churches to boast a fig tree growing out of its wall. Both the fig tree here and at St Newlyn

Surrounded by semitropical trees, Manaccan church has a fig tree growing from its wall.

East have a warning about their pruning in local gossip and legend — a terrible fate awaits anyone who dares to cut either of them! The south door is Norman and the original roofs remain. Visit the church during the local flower festival to witness a scene of great activity, beauty and fragrance.

Wandering round the hillside village of thatched cottages and pretty gardens, it is odd to think that Captain Bligh (of *The Bounty*) was mistakenly taken for a French spy here and arrested whilst doing some research for the admiralty. It was also near Manaccan that William Gregor discovered what he called Manaccanite, now known as Titanium. Provisions for your walk may be obtained at the Post Office, or you may care to preface your walk with a visit to the thatched New Inn. Excellent food is available here, but please remember — you have a six mile walk ahead of you!

Taking the lane to the east of the church, alongside the vicarage, you come to a footpath marked 'Carne' which leads you down hill, across fields. On reaching the wood the path forks. Take the right-hand path which leads, in the spring, down through woods of bluebells and wild garlic to a bridge over a stream and a tarmac road. Turn left and you soon reach the head of Gillan Creek, but instead of following the road to Carne, take the left turn alongside the creek as far as St Anthony-in-Meneage. If the tide is out you will be able to leave the road

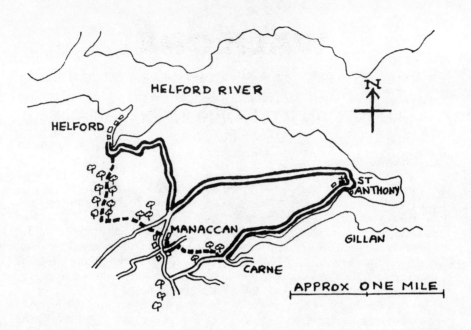

HELFORD RIVER

HELFORD

ST ANTHONY

MANACCAN

GILLAN

CARNE

APPROX ONE MILE

The New Inn at Manaccan — a good port of call at the start or the end of your walk.

The footpath leads downhill, across fields.

The head of Gillan Creek at low tide.

and walk along the beach as far as the church, and from this direction the tower is seen amidst a forest of masts of boats drawn up on the bank.

The 15th-century tower has battlements and pinnacles, and we were delighted to find the unusual lighting of many candelabra, with real candles, and a fine carving of the Last Supper on the Norman Font. Opposite, across the creek, is Gillan harbour — a busy port in medieval times with ships exporting fish, slate and tin, but now a favourite rendezvous for yachtsmen.

At this point we usually put our dog Tessa on her lead and plod up the tarmac road towards Manaccan, turning right before reaching the village and passing the entrance to Bosahan. A footpath then leads downhill into Helford village. This route gives wonderful views across Falmouth Bay to St Anthony Head on Zone Point ten miles away and also across to Durgan on the other side of the Helford River.

The more energetic could follow the coastal path all the way from St Anthony to Helford, passing the rocky outcrop known as The Gew

and the pretty riverside hamlet of Treath.

Helford is still one of our favourite villages and one which has reached a sensible compromise with traffic. It is discouraged but not forbidden and an ample car park copes with the summer tourist traffic.

The thatched Shipwright's Arms is our target for an excellent bar lunch, and if the weather is fine you can find a sheltered spot in the garden and enjoy one of the most pleasant estuary views in Cornwall. Across the creek is Treath and across the river the view stretches from Helford Passage to Toll Point. We have been here often and it is a favourite landfall for yachtsmen from Belgium and Brittany. There are always interesting people and boats to study and the houses along either side of the creek are picturesque at any time of year.

Daniel Defoe is said to have been inspired to write *Robinson Crusoe* while staying and listening to the yarns of local sailors.

An ancient path winds steeply up from the head of the village through deciduous woods and fields back to Manaccan. The faithful of

The 15th-century church tower at St Anthony, almost surrounded by ships' masts.

The roots of trees form strange shapes on the beach at St Anthony.

Helford, over the centuries, walked this path often as Manaccan was the nearest place of worship. Much of the walk is lined with towering beeches and bordered with ferns and flowers. It is a favourite section of the walk — also Tessa's judging by her terrific mileage in and out of the trees following scents.

There are many variations of this walk, depending on one's ability to walk and the time available. The New Inn at Manaccan has often provided us with a good bar lunch, and in Helford there is a cottage where one can savour wonderful jam and cream (and wasp!) teas in terraced gardens overlooking the river. When the season is right you can pick your own strawberries and raspberries at a farm near Manaccan. Last year we found a strawberry that would have won a prize at any garden show. This is a delightful walk which offers charming variations in scenery. There are also many places of interest in this historical part of Cornwall which has become a haven for yachtsmen and all those who seek peace and tranquility.

Thatched Helford cottages cluster together.

An ancient woodland path leads back up to Manaccan.

The old granite stile leading to Manaccan village.

WALK TWO

Peace, solitude and the sound of skylarks are some of the attractions of this walk to two of Cornwall's highest points.

ST BREWARD TO ROUGH TOR AND BROWN WILLY

OS Maps (1: 50,000) 200 & 201.
Length: approximately seven miles.

MOST Cornish folk and visitors have wanted to climb to the top of Brown Willy (1,377 feet, 420 metres) but comparatively few achieve this ambition. It is well worth the walk and subsequent climb as the view from the top on a clear day is breathtaking. On one occasion we could see Looe Island in one direction and the north coast near Hartland Point in the other.

Most people make their way to Brown Willy from the Camelford side (there is a car park at the end of a military road leading towards Rough Tor) or from A30 road near Bolventor and Jamaica Inn. Both are delightful walks, but I want to tell you of our favourite route from the area of St Breward. So let us start in that granite village, one of Cornwall's highest, on the northwestern fringes of Bodmin Moor.

The church at the centre of the village is mainly 15th century and is dedicated to a 13th-century Exeter bishop. Its tower, though not particularly tall, is visible for many miles. Nearby

The Old Granite Inn at St Breward — one of Cornwall's highest villages.

Pony and foal wander the moorland freely.

is The Old Inn with a granite-walled garden where we often stop for refreshment during our walks in this area. Before it stands a strangely inscribed stone. All around this parish are archaeological remains such as King Arthur's Hall, Bronze Age settlements, stone circles and burial mounds — in fact a real treasure area for those interested in ancient monuments.

Our walk can start from St Breward, but to shorten it we usually drive in a northerly direction to Tuckingmill, then easterly, round the base of Alex Tor along mainly unfenced road to a 'No Through Road' sign, passing a sign saying 'Rough Tor. 43rd Wessex Division War Memorial' and finally emerging into open moorland. The road is bordered by fir saplings on the right until you reach Camperdown Farm. Here you will find a sign which reads 'Private Access — No Admittance. Fernacre Farm' on a massive block of granite. Do not drive beyond this point. Here is absolute peace and a perfect

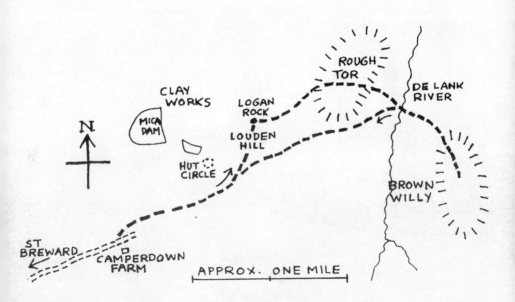

WC-B

place to start your walk. For those who are elderly or too young or perhaps disabled, this is the ideal place to have a picnic or a gentle walk up Alex Tor on one side of the track or to marvel at the 70-stone Bronze Age circle on the other side — towards Stannon Clay Works.

Depending on the time of year this walk is accompanied by a continual orchestra of sky-larks above, or cuckoos in late April; buzzards and crows frequently add their contribution. The only other sounds out here are of sheep, cattle, moorland ponies or the occasional distant chug of a tractor or bark of a dog.

Leaving the farm track on our right and with Tessa, our dachsund, doing her happiness dance of approval, we set off towards the great towering mass of Rough Tor, looking formid-able in the distance. If you walk across the springy turf in a direct line to the summit, you will first arrive at Louden Hill with its Logan Rock. Cornwall has many of these giant rocks, mainly of granite, so shaped by nature and the elements that by climbing on to the top and finding the exact position, they can be made to seesaw slowly and majestically. Desirée and Tessa joined me on the top and we rocked it successfully by just shifting our weight from one foot to another.

This is a wild spot and has vast horizons in all directions which made me think that Shelley had this sort of place in mind when he wrote:

"I love all waste and solitary places,
Where we taste
The pleasure of believing all we see
Is boundless, as we wish our soul to be."

For those of you who wish to include the climbing of Rough Tor (1,300 feet, 400 metres) in your walk, this is your moment of decision. From Louden Hill one walks to the top by climbing the northwestern side (the Camelford side) where one finds the bronze memorial tablet to the 43rd Wessex Division on the spot where there was once a little chapel dedicated to St Michael, the patron saint of high places.

A moorland walker tries out the Logan Rock on Louden Hill. In the background is Rough Tor.

The summit of Rough Tor is piled high with dramatic weather-sculpted rocks.

The peak Brown Willy and the bridge crossing the De Lank River.

Descending to the gate and bridge, follow the wall on the left for a while before striking off to your starting point.

Along the summit ridge of Rough Tor are the most incredible rock formations, the weathered granite forming beautifully sculpted shapes. There are also signs on the summit of stone enclosure walls joining some of the outcrops and dating from the Bronze Age, some 3,000 years ago. Descend the side of Rough Tor in a southeasterly direction to a little bridge at the valley bottom, between Rough Tor and Brown Willy.

For those who do not wish to climb Rough Tor, it is pleasant to walk from the Logan Rock direct to the bridge, skirting the southeastern side. The granite bridge crosses the De Lank River which here is just a fast running clear stream and the perfect place for a picnic and to cool off human feet. Tessa also decided it was a good place for a cooling swim. We were amazed at the tameness of the meadow pipits which pecked among the stones and peaty turf.

The path to the top of Brown Willy from here is well defined, zigzagging and steep, but well worth the climb. Standing on the roof of Cornwall by the cairn of stones and the Ordnance Survey triangulation pillar, the view is superb. A mile away to the north is Maiden Tor and the source of the River Fowey, and to the southwest you may see the sun reflected from the far distant traffic on the busy A30. To the southwest lies the lovely Garrow Tor, beyond which lies King Arthur's Hall. We were standing at this point last year on a hot August day watching and listening to summer storms all around us — black, ominous clouds and dramatic lightning — whilst we were in brilliant sunshine. Alas, we stayed too long and walked the last miles to the car in deluges of rain.

For the final stretch of this epic walk, follow the path back down to the bridge and head across the moor, keeping the farm track to your left. You will pass several late Bronze Age settlements and exposed burial mounds.

Seeing the moor in all its splendid desolation, it is hard to imagine a time when this was a relatively well-populated area with stone-walled round houses breaking the skyline near the foot of Louden Hill. On a hot day this can be quite an exhausting walk, so pick your weather carefully to avoid the likelihood of excess heat or driving mist. However, in the right weather it is a marvellously exhilarating experience.

The peat-stained waters of the De Lank River, just a stream at this point.

The summit of Brown Willy — Cornwall's highest point — 1,377 feet high.

The rocky ridge of Rough Tor faces you as you descend Brown Willy.

The remains of an early Bronze Age house on the desolate moorland.

WALK THREE

A coastal walk along high cliff-top paths and past secret rocky coves to a sheltered fishing village.

NARE HEAD TO PORTLOE

OS Map (1: 50,000) 204.
Length approximately four miles.

WE started this walk from the recently constructed National Trust car park near Nare Head. Because of the potential problem of congestion on the narrow lane leading to the headland, the National Trust has purposely not placed an inviting signpost on the main road from Veryan to Carne, thereby treating it as a place to discover rather than a main target for tourists.

To reach it, leave Veryan on the Portloe road and drive up the hillside to the crossroads. Turn right and travel about a quarter of a mile along the road towards Carne, where you will see a 'No Through Road' sign on the left. A short distance along this narrow lane you will find a car park, built on the site of a former farmhouse. A raised grassy platform reached by a ramp offers disabled people who wish to remain in their cars a spectacular view across the headland. The car park is also an ideal starting place for people seeking a fair-length coastal walk or wishing to walk just a short distance to Nare

The car park stile leading down to Kiberick Cove.

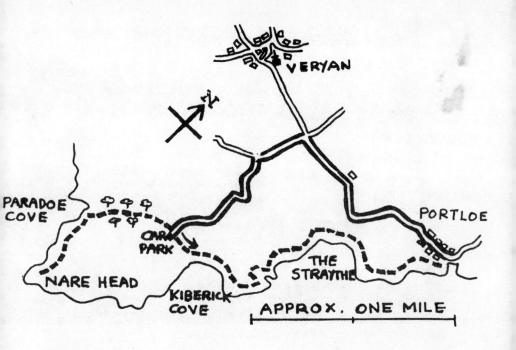

PARADOE
COVE

NARE HEAD

VERYAN

CAR
PARK

KIBERICK
COVE

THE
STRAYTHE

PORTLOE

APPROX. ONE MILE

Gull Rock, about a mile off Nare Head.

Bracken-clad cliffs surround The Straythe, halfway along the route.

Head itself — a walk I will describe later.

Across the road from the entrance to the car park is a three-step stile in the wall. Cross this and walk down across the sloping field to the coastal footpath and Kiberick Cove. From here you can look across Veryan Bay to Hemmick Beach and the Dodman, the highest point on Cornwall's south coast, topped by a granite cross. It was placed there in 1896 by a saintly man who was at that time vicar of St Michael and Caerhays and who was appalled at the many wrecks occurring on the rocks surrounding Dodman Point. Anne Treneer mentions him in her delightful book about her childhood nearby in the 1920s, *Schoolhouse in the Wind*.

Not quite a mile offshore from here is one of Cornwall's many Gull Rocks with the frightening Middle and Outer Stones showing just above the surface and a menace to the unwary mariner. Walking northeast along the coastal footpath you will see a host of wild flowers at any time

of the year — even in late autumn I have seen wild violets, buttercups and campions all within a hundred yards.

The path leads "up and down like a fiddler's elbow", and a steep descent across a field eventually takes you into another cove and across a couple of streams to a series of giant steps leading up the cliff for about 150 feet. They were obviously cut by a very large person and the top would have been a perfect place to find a seat (which we did not).

Every stile on this walk — and there are quite a few — is different in design and several are extremely picturesque and well made. The coastal path leads to the high cliffs above Portloe known as The Jakka. From here you can look down on the cottages straggling up the narrow valley and the little beach with fishing boats hauled to safety above the high-water mark. Portloe remains the perfect gem of a typical Cornish fishing village with the steep-sided valley

Paradoe Cove, a little-visited rocky inlet.

The sheltered fishing village of Portloe.

The blue waters of Gerrans Bay and Carne Beach seen from Nare Head.

carrying a stream past pretty cottages, pub, chapel and church, all on a diminutive scale. The church (All Saints) is as near the sea as one can get as it was once the lifeboat station, built in 1870 and housing a ten-oared boat called *Gorfenkle* after the man who gave both boat and house to Portloe. In 1877 a new lifeboat house was built close to what is now the excellent Lugger Hotel, run by the Powell family. A great number of Portloe folk are distantly related and it seems to me that most people are named either Jones or Trudgeon.

After exploring the village, take the tarmac road up the hill past the pleasant Ship Inn (where you may obtain a bar lunch) and turn right along a footpath marked 'To Veryan', past a charming group of cottages and well-tended gardens. An uphill walk across fields leads you to a five-step stile. Turn right and continue in a westerly direction until you reach a crossroads where you turn left. After less than a mile you will find yourself back at the entrance to the narrow lane leading to the Nare Head car park.

For those of you who want a shorter walk (or still have the energy to walk a little further) cross the stile near the rear of the car park marked 'To Paradoe Cove and Nare Head'. Walk straight ahead down the right-hand side of the field and cross a small stile into a wooded valley. The walk from here down to the beach is delightful — through woodland of fir, oak, mountain ash and beech giving way to bracken as you reach a peaceful rocky cove. To reach Nare Head itself, follow the track up alongside a ruined cottage to a welcome seat at the top of the headland. From here it is a short stroll to the gorse-fringed

Paradoe Cove with the path up to Nare Head on the left.

tip of Nare Head. The view on a clear day is magnificent — right across Gerrans Bay to Portscatho and further down the coast to the Manacles and the spire of St Keverne church. Inland you may be able to make out the giant dishes of Goonhilly and the television mast at Carnkie, near Redruth.

We were once here in darkness and could identify the flashing light of the Eddystone lighthouse just below the horizon.

The path back to the car park seems very leisurely compared to the stiff climb up to the headland, and it is one of the most pleasant short walks I know.

Portscatho, across Gerrans Bay.

A stream runs through well-tended gardens at the head of the village.

WALK FOUR

A walk through woodland bordering two of
Cornwall's most beautiful rivers.
ST WINNOW TO LERRYN.
OS Map (1: 50,000) 200.
Length: approximately seven miles.

THIS is a walk we have done many times; a walk of interest, beauty and tranquility and one of which we could never tire.

St Winnow is best reached from Lostwithiel — take the first road on the right to the east of the old bridge over the River Fowey. Narrow lush green lanes overhung with trees and bordered with ferns and red campion lead downhill to the riverside church. The vicar of St Winnow, Canon Miles Brown, is an old friend and a distinguished scholar, priest, civil engineer, historian, clock-maker and organ-builder. His notice on the door of the church is so refreshing and welcoming:

"Welcome, friends, from here and there.
Never mind the clothes you wear.
God looks upon the inward heart,
Worship Him — in peace depart."

There was another kindly welcome for us in Mr Stephens' St Winnow Barton Farm Museum near the church. It is a fascinating and free exhibition of what I might describe as 'Agriculture Through the Ages' and delighted us with such items as a 1890 bruising mill and 1900 tyre bender. I wonder how many visitors would be able to describe double whippletrees, maize breakers, reed combers, sheep couplers, trap-

The Church of St Winnow on the banks of the River Fowey. The walls are Norman and the tower and roofs date from the 1480s. The gate leading to the foreshore is at the far side of the churchyard, behind the church.

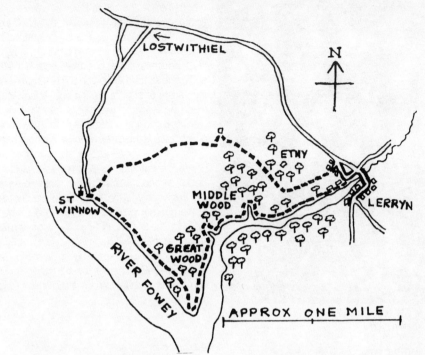

per's hammers, a giant swill ladle, a washing dolly, eel shears, salmon spears, a rick thatcher's butting board, a seed barrow, a milk hopper, a cake breaker or a corn crusher?

The third welcome was from three swans flying upstream and landing to join a dozen others just opposite us as we stood in the churchyard. One tombstone from 1902 told us of the death of someone at the Earl Chatham, Bridgend, and this puzzled me until I noticed an inn of this name on our way home, near the 15th-century bridge in Lostwithiel. The name derives from the owner of the nearby great house and estate of Boconnoc, the first William Pitt, who took the title of Lord Chatham.

St Winnow has been a holy place since about AD 670 when St Winnoc set up a thatched cob oratory: he did likewise in Brittany at Plouhinec and near Dunkirk at Berrges-St Vinoc. One of the church windows depicts him carrying a handmill — his saintly symbol. The east window has some 16th-century glass, giving information on the fashionable dress of the period, and the restored rood screen and pulpit date from 1520. The bench ends are full of interest and we saw a fine carving of a ship and another of a Cornishman in a kilt — common dress at the time. We noticed an epitaph (from 1651) of one William Sawle in the Lady Chapel:

"When I was sick, most men did deem me ill.
If I had lived, I should have been so still.
Praise be the Lord, that in the Heavens doth dwell,
Who has received my soul — now I am well."

More recently millions of television viewers all over the world saw a 1780 wedding staged at the little church in the BBC production of Winston Graham's *Poldark* series. How well chosen, we thought as we left the churchyard by the little gate in the far corner, alongside the

The bench end depicting a kilted Cornishman taking a drink.

woods beside the broad River Fowey before turning northwards, following the tortuous bends of the River Lerryn. This is a delightful part of the walk, the path winding beneath ancient oaks, beeches, sweet chestnut and ash trees, and if you sit for a while you will be amazed at the variety of bird life around you. When you reach the second of two creeks, take the lower path down to the right before the main track which follows the creek up to St Winnow Mill.

Shortly after passing over a small wooden bridge, the path returns to the riverside at Ethy Rocks, a good spot for a picnic. I like to believe that this wood was the 'Wild Wood' of Kenneth Graham's marvellous book, *The Wind in the Willows*, the first part of which he wrote whilst staying at the Green Bank Hotel, Falmouth. In my imagination I can see him with his friend, Sir Arthur Quiller-Couch ('Q'), rowing or sailing over from Fowey and walking or picnicking along this stretch.

river. After passing a boathouse we made our way downstream along the foreshore, ducking under or climbing over the mooring ropes of boats.

A few hundred yards along the beach a little stream indicates where you have to negotiate a very wet patch through stinging nettles and thorns to a stile, into a field, and then by another to the beginnings of Great Wood. The entry from fields to wood is easily missed, as we found to our cost many years ago, so look out for a low hedge and a footpath sign. Just as we were about to enter the trees we heard a rumbling sound from across the river and were amazed to see two locomotives hauling 44 wagons of china clay down to the docks at Fowey. This railway track, running right alongside the river from Lostwithiel, must surely be one of the most beautiful stretches in the West Country.

The footpath leads southeast through the

A bridge leads you across the stream at the head of Tregays Creek.

Ethy Rocks — an ideal spot for a picnic.

Mr and Mrs Bennetts at the gate of Creek Cottage.

...he stile leading to the high footpath back across the fields.

Shortly after passing an old mill on the far bank, the village of Lerryn comes into view and you pass idyllically situated cottages covered with clematis and wisteria. The path turns left, past a row of charming white cottages, then right and past a green house, leading to the 15th-century bridge, the village proper and the Ship Inn. We avoided the stepping stones over the river as we did not feel we should be quite as welcome with a hot, wet and muddy dog! The landlord was, in fact, very welcoming and soon we tucked into an excellent bar lunch.

Wandering round the village with its delightful riverside cottage, one general store and ivy-covered limekiln, we made our way back to Creek Cottage beside the bridge, the home of Mr and Mrs Bennetts. She was born here 78 years ago and they had just celebrated 56 years of obviously happy married life. They were kind

The granite bridge of the River Fowey was built 500 years ago. At low tide you may cross by stepping stones.

The welcoming Ship Inn near the quayside at Lerryn.

St Winnow church seen across fields on the return walk.

enough to show us round their beautiful garden running down to the river. The trees were all hung with flowering honeysuckle and clematis and all the nesting boxes appeared to be occupied. Mr Bennetts told us a charming story of the box he made for the garden gate to receive the daily 'pintas'. One day he found it was the chosen home of some great tits, so he told the milkman not to use it for a while and the rearing of the young birds continued. It was a privilege to meet such a happy, contented couple.

We returned to the bridge and, sitting for a while looking downstream, we noticed swallows sweeping low over the water and several kingfishers, darting like blue bullets along the bank. An ancient earthwork stretches from Lerryn right across to Looe — although it takes quite an effort to find many parts of it now. It has puzzled people for centuries, hence the old saying: "One day the devil, having nothing to do, built a great hedge from Lerryn to Looe." However, Craig Weatherhill in his book *Cornovia* suggests that it was a Dark Age territorial boundary.

If you wish to return to St Winnow by a different route, retrace your steps as far as the green house and turn right at the row of white cottages, following the steep lane up as far as a road called Lerryn View on your left. Walk through the estate and at the far end you will find a stile tucked away behind the last bungalow on the right. From here a path leads across high rolling farmland, with fine views down into the river valley, back to St Winnow.

However if, like us, you enjoyed the outward section of the walk, why not retrace your steps alongside the river.

WALK FIVE

Along green lanes and cliff-tops to one of Cornwall's finest vantage points.
MORVAH TO PENDEEN WATCH
OS Map (1: 50,000) 203.
Length: approximately five miles.

WHEN my wife and I want a day of 'solitude and sea' we make for the little granite church of Morvah, midway between St Ives and Land's End on the busy winding B3306. The 600-year-old church stands surrounded by farms and barns between the high moorland of Carn Downs and the Atlantic, 400 feet below. Inside the church the Swedish flag is much in evidence as it shares its dedication with Sweden's patron saint. An unusual little treasure (known locally as 'The Iceberg', I'm told) rests on a rather precarious stand and takes the form of a sculptured glass ornament with the outline of the church and its squat tower etched within. It was presented to the Church of St Bridget by the Swedish manager of Dartington Glass. Mr Mann, the owner of Merthyr Farm, opposite the church, explained the origins of a large round stone by his gate which I took to be part of a corn mill. It was in fact originally laid flat and used for binding wooden wheels, the hole at its centre being for the wheel's hub.

To the right of the church and through two gates, a brambly path or green lane winds between fields, heading north towards the sea. As the land slopes away, following the valley down to the coastal footpath, it becomes rather

Morvah village and church. On the left is the old Board School, built in 1882.

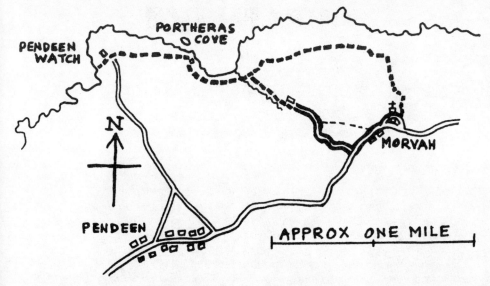

Portheras Cove showing the path winding along the headland to Boat Cove and the lighthouse.

The rocky gulley at the head of Portheras Cove. Beyond is Boat Cove.

muddy underfoot — so step carefully. On joining the coastal path, head westwards past Greeb Point and along the cliff top. We once stopped to watch a kestrel here — not hovering but remaining equally static simply by riding the updraught from the cliff's edge. The path winds through bracken, gorse and heather down into a steep gully; the path to the left is the one we will be taking later back to Morvah. But for the moment, turn right into the gulley where a gushing waterfall plunges into a small pool before winding between the rocks onto the beach of Portheras Cove. Until recently the steel ribs of the tragic wreck of the *Alacrity* could be seen on the beach here.

Our next port of call is Boat Cove, a small collection of fishermen's huts on the far left rim of Portheras Cove. If the tide is low you can

The waterfall and pool at the mouth of the valley.

Boat Cove, a sheltered refuge for north coast fishermen.

reach it by walking across the flat sand, but at high tide you should cross the stream and follow the coastal path up the hillside and down to the cove. I was fascinated by the clever device for hauling up the fishing boats, the motive power being a small stationary engine. We have happy memories of family picnics here with carrycots and all the other paraphernalia of small children and dogs.

You will already have noticed the tip of Pendeen Lighthouse peeking over the headland of Pendeen Watch. It is reached by a short walk up the coastal path — but before you enter, carry on past its rear for a most dramatic view along the coast as far as Cape Cornwall. This sight is best seen during a storm with the smoky spray of crashing waves outlining the various headlands. If the weather is unsuitable for walking, you can drive to this point and safely enjoy the power and beauty of a winter storm.

Pendeen Lighthouse was built in 1900 and has a two-million-candlepower lamp flashing four white flashes every 15 seconds. "Four every 15 — it must be Pendeen" is the easily remembered phrase by which the light is recognised. Its powerful fog signal sounds for two seconds every 20 seconds in foul weather, and it is not hard to imagine that the full force of an Atlantic gale must be a terrifying experience. Andy Bluer, Principal Keeper of Pendeen Light and one of four keepers who maintain the interior mechanism in spotless condition, told us that the light can be seen for about 30 miles. He explained that there had probably been a watch kept on this headland since the days when the barbarians sailed down the coast to raid the crops of nearby settlements at Chûn.

Our route back to Morvah follows the path back to the waterfall behind Portheras Cove, then directly inland and up the valley lane for

The mighty foghorns and light at Pendeen Watch.

The lenses which magnify the light to two-million candlepower.

Ancient granite hedges topped by gorse.

Principal Keeper of the Pendeen Light, Andy Bluer, has been in the service of Trinity House for over 30 years.

a short distance. If you wish you may return to Morvah via a medieval church path, as 'straight as a die' across the fields and over lovely old stiles. Alternatively you may follow the lane to the main road and turn left for the village. The ancient granite hedges along this route are magnificent and the result of fields being hard won from the rock-strewn landscape.

I have described only one walk from here, but others abound if you are interested in some of Cornwall's archaeological treasures, all within the parish boundaries. These include the second-century Chûn Castle and Chûn Quoit high on the moors overlooking Morvah, and the small holed stone of the Mên-an-Tol and the nearby standing stone of Mên Scryfa, marking the sixth-century burial place of Rialobran, the Royal Raven.

Looking south from Pendeen Watch to Cape Cornwall, past the engine houses of Levant and Botallack.

WALK SIX

A walk for all seasons, from moorland lakeside to valley waterfalls.

SIBLYBACK LAKE TO GOLITHA FALLS

OS Map (1: 50,000) 201.
Length: Approximately eight miles.

W E started this walk from the extensive car park on the east side of Siblyback Lake, north of St Cleer. It is signposted on the road from Doublebois to Minions.

We always regard this man-made lake and reservoir as an asset to Bodmin Moor as, apart from its main purpose, it is picturesque and provides plenty of recreational opportunities such as windsurfing, angling, sailing and birdwatching. A great variety of birds visit the lake throughout the year, including a small wintering flock of smew. Below the car park is a discreet clubhouse and small cafeteria.

The lake is something comparatively new to those of us familiar with the magnificent view from the top of Kilmar Tor in the far distance, but it adds its own beauty to the area. The car park is an ideal spot to bring the elderly or disabled as there is plenty to watch on the lake against a beautiful background.

Siblyback Lake, looking south from the car park.

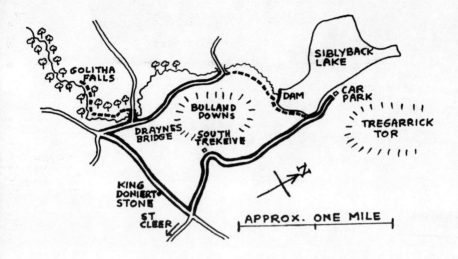

GOLITHA FALLS

SIBLYBACK LAKE

DAM

CAR PARK

BULLAND DOWNS

TREGARRICK TOR

DRAYNES BRIDGE

SOUTH TREKEIVE

KING DONIERT STONE

ST CLEER

APPROX. ONE MILE

The clubhouse and cafeteria at Siblyback.

WC-D

The mighty wall of Siblyback dam, with Tregarrick Tor beyond.

Draynes Bridge across the River Fowey.

We walked to the dam itself by way of a lakeside path running south from the car park. It passes many small sandy beaches before reaching the mighty dam wall. A seemingly endless flight of steps just before the dam leads down to the water-treatment plant with the smooth walls now towering above you. Follow the path to Trekeivesteps which winds through bracken and gorse before reaching a minor metalled road where you turn left. It is a pleasant walk downhill from here with sheep grazing to your left and a deep valley to your right. On our last visit we stopped to watch a large buzzard circling slowly overhead, quartering the fields in search of prey.

After the bare moorland heights surrounding Siblyback Lake, the valley trees provide a pleasant contrast. Just before reaching Draynes Bridge a footpath leads off to the left around the base of the hill, but it is advisable not to take this as the way is extremely boggy at the far end.

Cascading water at Golitha Falls.

Moorland sheep near Redgate.

Draynes Bridge was built for packhorses in the 15th century and is one of the many attractive crossings of the River Fowey. We will see some more further down the river on Walk Ten. The walk downstream from here is dazzlingly beautiful at any time of year. In the spring patches of bluebells and daffodils border the rushing water and in the summer and autumn you walk beneath the green and bronze leaves of towering beech trees. Even during the winter months, the colourful fallen leaves and mossy boulders in mid-river contrast with the white gushing water forming a delightful scene. The path meets many little streams flowing into the River Fowey and these we usually negotiate by stepping stones, footbridges or just by leaping.

As you progress downstream you will be aware that the sound of water pouring over rocks is getting louder as the gradient increases. These are Golitha Falls, a series of small waterfalls and gorges with grassy banks suitable for picnics in solitude, with sight and sound fully occupied.

Our pleasure on one particular day was enhanced by the chance meeting with a group of mentally handicapped young people who were enjoying a day's excursion with a spontaneous joy and innocence that we found quite infectious. What a fuss they made of our little dog who did quite a few miles playing 'catch-me-if-you-can' in and out of the trees. In the course of this both dog and children became pretty wet, but happy. Incidentally, I understand the correct pronunciation of Golitha is not with an 'eye' in the middle, but 'Goleetha'.

After returning to Draynes Bridge over the roots of trees jutting through their carpet of leaves, turn right and walk to the Doublebois to Minions road, where you should turn left, heading roughly east. After about half a mile you will come to King Doniert's Stone, re-erected here some years ago by the local Old

Mushroom stones at South Trekeive.

Cornwall Society. Doniert was the 9th-century King of East Cornwall who drowned just half a mile away. Two pieces of the stone are preserved and one bears the latin inscription DONIERT ROGAVIT PRO ANIMA — 'Doniert ordered this for his soul'. The other stone is decorated with a panel of interlaced carving.

Continuing eastwards you will soon reach the road on your left that leads you back to the car park. As you pass through the small farming hamlet of South Trekeive you may wish to stop at The Shippen for a cream tea — during the season — and to admire the collection of mushroom stones in a roadside garden. The largest one, the owner Mrs Wall told us, was formed by a millstone on top of a cricket pitch roller! Her husband, Peter, was one of the men who helped build the dam we saw earlier.

From here it is a short stroll along the lane to the lakeside and the reservoir car park. We have done this walk at all times of the year in all weathers and found it equally beautiful, each season lending it a special quality.

King Doniert's Stone in its roadside enclosure. (Photograph by Craig Weatherhill.)

WALK SEVEN

Ancient stiles, peaceful streamside lanes, honey for sale
and even a day's fishing form part of the walk from
PERRANZABULOE TO BOLINGEY
OS Map (1: 50,000) 204.
Length: Approximately five and a half miles.

THIS walk is very well known to us as it starts from my daughter's home close to Perranzabuloe parish church which is on the A3075 road, about two miles southeast of Perranporth. Perhaps the name should give a clue as to the church's history for the word means 'St Piran's-in-the-sands'. It is in fact the third parish church as the first two were over-

The Church of St Piran, Perranzabuloe. An illustration by Alice Bizley on the cover of the excellent church guide.

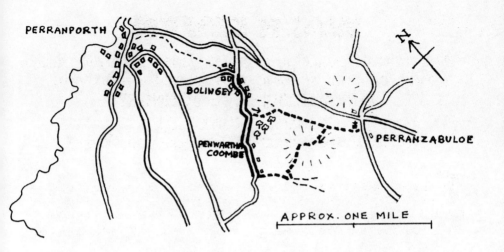

whelmed by sand. The first one was a little oratory of the sixth century which was abandoned because of drifting dunes in the 11th century, rediscovered in 1835 and covered with a concrete shell, and in 1980 sadly reburied in the sand. The second church was Norman and built close to the first one, but this was abandoned in 1804, dismantled stone by stone and rebuilt further inland where we find it today. One can find the site of that second church — and it is a favourite summer stroll for us — marked by a nine-feet-high cross, carved in the tenth century with only three holes instead of the usual four carved into its head. Inside the present church is an octagonal font and some interesting slate memorials and carved wooden panels. A strange face peers down at you from above the porch. An excellent little church guide, written by the late Maurice Bizley and charmingly illustrated by his wife, Alice, is on sale in the church. A collection of church guides purchased throughout the county can act as informative as well as evocative souvenirs of country walks.

Lone Lane — bordered with primroses in spring.

Many old stiles stand alongside gates on this walk

Penwartha Coombe school, now a private dwelling, at the foot of Lone Lane.

Many charming cottages in Penwartha Coombe are reached by crossing small bridges.

Bolingey Lake, open for fishing all the year round.

To begin this walk, follow the churchyard path west of the church, past the green gate to the rectory and down into a narrow lane, known locally as Lone or Slads Lane. In springtime this has a 'fairy-glen' atmosphere with the hedges a mass of primroses, bluebells, campions and wild violets. This path leads up over a stone stile and through a wooden gate to higher ground from where you get a fine view of distant cliffs and white surf. Looking at the encroaching sand north of Perranporth it is easy to realise why the church was moved so far inland at the third attempt.

Heading due west, ancient stiles lead us across fields and downhill into another lovely lane — Love Lane — with a stream running alongside and often rather muddy. Do *not* cross the small stone bridge, but turn right and walk downhill into Penwartha Coombe. The house on the corner was once the village school and we now turn right along the valley with the sound of the stream beside us until we reach Bolingey.

At places such as Nanslade Mill and other attractive properties alongside the road, notice the advantage of having a garden with a stream running through it and having little bridges to the front door.

Just before reaching Trevellance Cottage you will notice, on your right, a vertical post marked Cox Hill leading to a small bridge and footpath. This is your route back to Perranzabuloe, but first, continue along the valley to the charming village of Bolingey.

Shortly before reaching the village inn, where you can enjoy a good bar lunch, you pass Bolingey Lake, a four-and-a-half acre fishing lake created by Bill Phillips and open all the year round. It is stocked with perch, tench, roach and carp and day tickets are available.

Bolingey Inn, a good resting place at the halfway stage of the walk.

The old riverside mill in the valley below Bolingey chapel.

Bolingey is a most picturesque and unspoilt village and contains one of the most attractive thatched houses in the West Country. It is a good place to buy local honey, and up Chapel Hill there is usually a good selection of bedding plants for sale — especially fuchsias. A narrow lane opposite the Methodist chapel meanders past cottages and houses all the way to Perranporth. Should you wish to follow this path on some occasion you will pass the original GWR station which I remember being very busy in summertime, with horsedrawn carriages in the station forecourt.

As you will no doubt wish to return to Perranzabuloe to pick up your transport, retrace your steps through Bolingey and along the valley to Trevellance Cottage, where you turn left by the sign to Cox Hill, across the bridge, over a stile and up across the fields almost to your starting point — at the head of Lone Lane near the church.

This is just one of many hundred walks in this large parish of 11,000 acres, and 13 of them are described in a little booklet called *Perran Paths*, compiled and published by the Perranzabuloe Old Cornwall Society.

An attractive thatched house at the foot of Chapel Hill.

WALK EIGHT

Besides the reedy river banks of the River Hayle and along narrow lanes winding through rolling farmland.

ST ERTH TO RELUBBUS

OS Map (1: 50,000) 203.
Length: Approximately six miles.

SOMETIMES it is useful to know where to take a pleasant stroll without hills, for friends or relatives who are too old, too young or perhaps disabled. The secret is to find somewhere away from the 'madding crowd' and thus I suggest you make for Hayle and from its centre follow the signposts to St Erth, leaving your car by the church. Alternatively, you could catch the train to St Erth station and walk the short distance into the village.

We find that the pace of life comes to an 'emergency halt' here and does not resume for the rest of the day. This holy place was founded in 500 AD by St Ercus, one of three missionaries who came over from Ireland, the other two being St Ia (St Ives) and St Uny (Lelant). Unlike his sister Ia, who is reputed to have sailed to Cornwall on a leaf, Ercus is said to have travelled on a millstone!

We love our visits to the church at St Erth with its 15th-century tower and even earlier parts. A stained-glass window in the south wall depicts Bishop Benson, Truro's first bishop, holding a model of Truro cathedral in his hand. One of the benchends has the figure of a Truro bishop of 1912, Bishop Stubbs. On the wall is a great wooden letter of thanks from King Charles I in Sudely Castle, in which he thanks the Cornish for their loyalty during the Civil War. Only a comparatively few survive now, but at one time there was one in practically every church in Cornwall.

The Church of St Ercus, beautifully restored by J D Sedding in 1873.

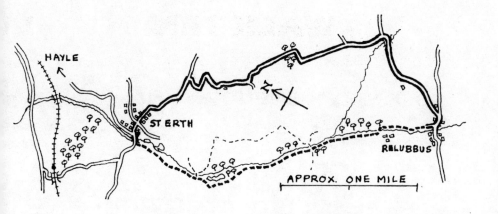

Large trading ships once sailed up to the bridge at St Erth.

The centre of St Erth with its granite cross alongside the store.

The peaceful banks of the River Hayle.

Trout dart from beneath waving waterweed.

The village pump outside the converted chapel.

St Erth suffered a cholera outbreak in 1832 and the mass grave of unnamed victims is in the graveyard.

What a surprise we had when we came to the lychgate given in memory of the Vivian family of Hayle. It was to this family that my mother came as a nurse from her native Wales and where she met my father. I also remember that my late brother and I were trusted at the age of seven and nine to travel by GWR from Truro to Hayle to be met by the Misses Vivian, whose guests we were for the day.

At one time ships came right up to the medieval bridge close to the church. Built in the 14th century, the bridge has many arches, but as the river silted up, most of them became engulfed and only four spans remain visible.

Cross the bridge over the River Hayle and immediately pick up a riverside path that meanders upstream through reed beds, water meadows and past pools and an occasional cottage. Although quite narrow — little more than a gushing stream — the waterway is often quite deep and dark, with skeins of red and

St Erth church, seemingly rising from the reeds.

One of several ancient thatched cottages in Relubbus.

The bridge at Relubbus. The path along which you have walked can be seen on the right.

green waterweed waving in the current. Trout dart away at your approach and there is a rich variety of birdlife attracted by the water. I was reminded of the upper reaches of the Wiltshire Avon with its wealth of wild flowers, birds of all types — including herons — and general air of tranquillity.

One can walk upstream as far as one's energy allows, but our favourite walk leads us about two and a half miles to the little hamlet of Relubbus on the B3280 road that runs from Marazion to Leedstown. Just before reaching this road, at a point where the path crosses the river to the northeast bank, you pass a beautifully sited caravan leisure park, a small working waterwheel and a working windmill. It is always interesting to see that there really are people who are obviously aware of nature's ability to provide cheap energy.

Relubbus is a village of pretty cottages, some very old and thatched. The chapel has been tastefully converted into two houses and the owner hopes to repair the pump that stands by the roadside. We usually call in at Mr and Mrs

The return walk along the valley side passes through rich, rolling farmland.

Hosker's post office and general stores for a bite to eat before returning to St Erth. In springtime, the fields above and surrounding Relubbus are bright with daffodils.

You may wish to return to St Erth 'on the flat' by retracing your steps along the riverside walk, but if you can manage some gentle hills, you might like to return by way of lanes which follow the high eastern side of the valley. To take this route, pass the post office and walk uphill, turning first left up Gurlyn Hill and walking to the top. The lane descends and at the valley bottom, close to a small stream, turn left and walk along Countess Bridge Lane. At the first junction walk straight ahead along the same

lane between fields of cabbages and down into a valley and across a small ford.

The lane now turns sharply right and left through a wood of ancient beech and oak trees, alive with squirrels and wood pigeons. Turn right at the next junction and walk along Porthcollum Lane until it reaches the road climbing out of St Erth. Turn left here and descend into the village, passing an estate, a charming terrace of cottages, the Star Inn and the village's old stone cross alongside the village store.

This is a gentle walk, away from noise and bustle, and I suggest you allow its peace to envelop you as you walk further and further upstream and return along little-used lanes.

71

WALK NINE

A walk through Thomas Hardy Country, from Paradise beside sparkling waters to three small country churches.
BOSCASTLE AND THE VALENCY VALLEY
OS Map (1: 50,000) 190.
Length: Approximately ten miles.

THIS walk is best enjoyed in spring and autumn. It starts from the large car park at the head of the village. The steep descent into Boscastle from the south is through the aptly named area known as Paradise — a straggle of interesting buildings on many levels. Here also is the Napoleon Inn where soldiers were recruited during the Napoleonic Wars. Down in the village alongside the Old Mill is another reminder of those times — the Wellington Hotel.

Before starting the walk you will probably wish to explore the village and wander past the old slate buildings and cottages down by the harbour. The narrow hidden entrance to the harbour must have been a real hazard to mariners of old under sail in a gale, and for many years rowing boats known as hobblers were used to guide vessels through the narrow cleft in the cliffs.

The tiny pier was built by the famous Cornish sailor, Sir Richard Grenville, in the 16th century

The 16th-century pier and sheltered harbour at Boscastle.

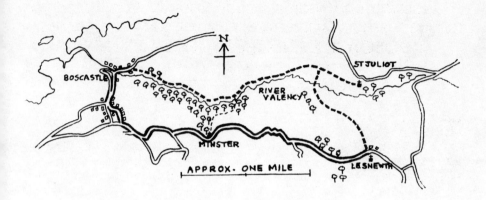

and was used for the export of Delabole slate and for fishing.

Back at the National Trust car park alongside the Cobweb Inn — a warm friendly place where good food can be obtained — our walk leads inland from the village and up the Valency valley. A gate at the eastern end of the car park allows access to meadows and a wood where the path runs beside the sparkling, fast-flowing Valency River, alive with trout and its own music.

The path snakes along beside the river, beneath high rocky crags and steep valley sides for about two and a half miles before gently climbing the north side to St Juliot's church. Marked but not named on the OS map, it is known by the locals as 'St Jilt'. It is associated professionally and romantically with Thomas Hardy for it was here that he came in 1870 in his capacity as an architect to restore the church and stayed to woo and marry his first wife, Emma Gifford, in 1874.

Slate houses and cottages line the banks of the Valency river as it winds through the village.

The riverside footpath, bordered with wild flowers in spring and summer.

The interior of St Juliot church, restored by Thomas Hardy in 1872.

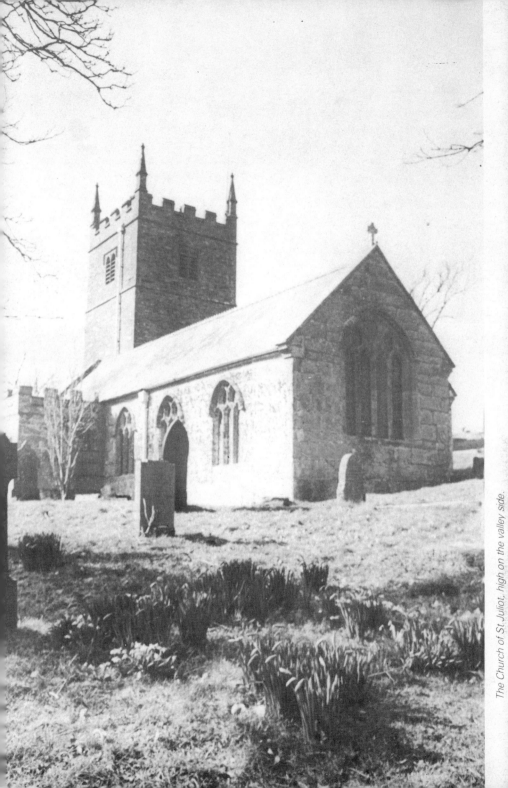

The Church of St. Juliot, high on the valley side.

The wide sweep of the Valency Valley seen from St Juliot Church.

Hardy loved this valley and one can identify St Nectan's Kieve (in the next valley) in *Under the Waterfall*, and Beeny Cliff, near Boscastle, in his poems. The whole area is described in his novel *A Pair of Blue Eyes*. There is a memorial to Emma Gifford, sister-in-law of the local rector, in the church. When we were there last, the churchyard was a mass of snowdrops and daffodils.

After enjoying a short rest we retraced our steps for about half a mile into the valley bottom and crossed the river where we were welcomed at the old farm by a horse, a pony, four dogs and a delightful lady. By way of a rural footbridge we then climbed up through the farm, tacking a track southeast to the village of Lesnewth. The church here is built in a fold in the side of the valley and only the top of the tower is visible until you enter the churchyard. The Courtyard Cottages opposite the church date from the 17th century; they were built as a mill for grinding and storing corn and grain from the surrounding area. They have been tastefully converted into dwellings and retain their charming character.

From Lesnewth head west along narrow minor roads which rise and fall steeply, through the hamlet of Treworld to the little church of Minster (again it is marked but not named on the OS map). It is built in a deep natural amphitheatre alongside the road and must be one of most beautifully-sited churches in Cornwall. We were lucky to be here once in daffodil time when the churchyard is one mass of blooms, planted originally by a former vicar during the 1914-18 war. The church is on the site of an ancient priory but is itself six centuries old and the mother church of Boscastle. On the west face of the tower is a carving pair of scissors — was it perhaps a mason's mark?

76

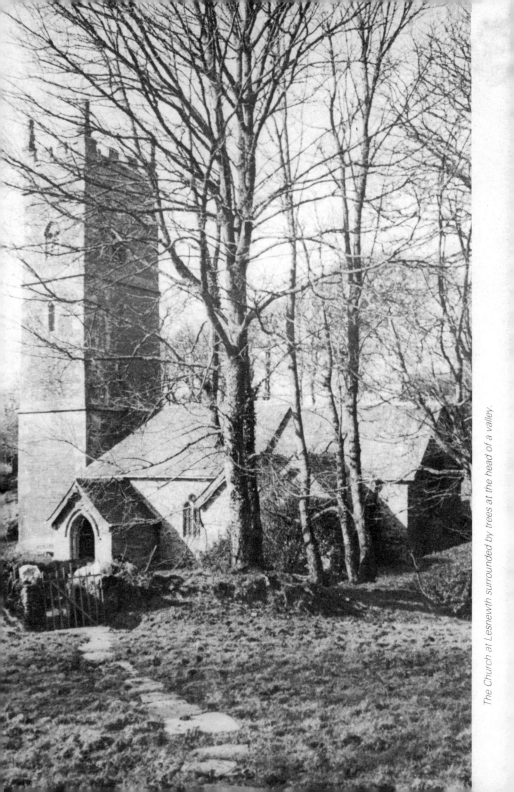

The Church at Lesnewth surrounded by trees at the head of a valley.

The little church at Minster, almost hidden in a deep amphitheatre.

Within the peace and quiet of the church we saw a tiny brass commemorating a child who died in the 16th century; there is also a touching inscription that tells us a lot about a happy marriage of 40 years in the 17th century. Apparently William Cotton's wife died first and then:

"She first departing, he a few weeks tried
To live without her: could not and so died."

From Minster you may either descend through Peter's Wood into the valley again to return to Boscastle, or continue west along the narrow road for a while before turning steeply downwards, over a stile and along a medieval path through fields and coppices into the village.

Our final bonus the last time we did this walk was seeing the point beyond the harbour bathed in soft evening sunlight, before receiving a warm welcome at the Valency House Hotel close to the harbour, and enjoying freshly cooked shortbread and tea in the lounge beside a fire.

Do try this walk 'out of season' and when you feel in need of peace and beauty.

The restored mill and part of the courtyard of charming buildings at Lesnewth.

WALK TEN

Using the railway, we find a cross-country walk along a wooded valley.

FOLLOWING THE RIVER FOWEY TO LOSTWITHIEL

OS Map (1: 50,000) 200.
Length: Approximately four and a half miles.

IN describing some of our favourite walks we have assumed that you arrive at the starting point by car, but for this final walk we have used the railway to arrive at our starting point — Bodmin Parkway station — returning home by train from Lostwithiel.

It will prove useful to check times of arrival and departure before leaving home, especially as regards Lostwithiel as fewer trains stop there.

On the 'down' side of the station at Bodmin Parkway the signal box has been transformed into a friendly little cafe — a good place to stock up with Mars bars before setting off. As you leave the station on this side turn right. Two tracks face you — one up to the left and one to the car park. Between them there is a small red gate which leads you to a leafy path that winds, under the railway and between laurel bushes to the banks of the River Fowey.

Cross the river by a small bridge and follow its general direction downstream with meadows on one side and woodland on the

The beautiful Glynn valley, near Bodmin Parkway station.

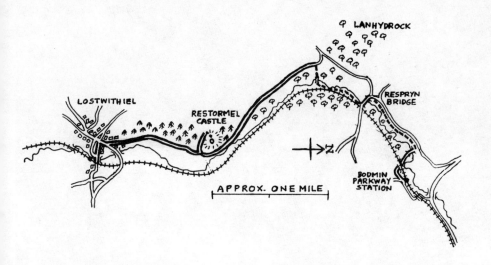

The River Fowey, winding beneath trees and dappled sunshine.

Respryn Bridge, one of the oldest in Cornwall.

The wooden stile alongside Respryn Bridge.

The keep of Restormel Castle on its imposing hilltop site.

other. This picturesque stretch of river belongs to the National Trust and day tickets for fishing are available (on the production of a South West Water Authority licence) from the National Trust Estate Office at nearby Lanhydrock. The NT also produces an interesting map of this stretch of river, naming the various pools and woods, for members of the Lanhydrock Angling Association.

Passing the peaceful waters of Corner Pond and Claypipe Pool you will arrive at a picnic area and car park adjacent to beautiful Respryn Bridge. Is this Cornwall's most painted bridge, I wonder?

It is only a short walk from the bridge to Lanhydrock House itself, and you may wish to incorporate a visit into your walk. The best time to see the gardens here is April and May when the glory of the long established camellias, azaleas and rhododendrons is quite breath-taking. Incidentally, you can have an excellent lunch or tea in the old servant's quarters of the house. It was, of course, mostly rebuilt in 1881 after a disastrous fire that left only the 1651 north wing and gatehouse intact. Its history is interesting in that it was held by the Royalists in the Civil War, whereas Lostwithiel a few miles away was a Cromwellian stronghold.

Resuming our walk at Respryn Bridge, cross the river, turn right over a wooden stile and follow the riverside path on the east bank. Sheltered by trees whose roots snake over the footpath, the river is at its most tranquil and beautiful along this stretch. We noted a couple of herons and some kingfishers and squirrels before reaching Kathleen Bridge, a well-made affair constructed by the National Trust, which carries you back to the west bank of the River Fowey.

Turn left and follow the path as it climbs away from the river to a lane which meanders along the valleyside towards Restormel Castle and Lostwithiel. The valley soon broadens out and the gently sloping contours are dotted with trees

The 15th-century bridge and quiet town of Lostwithiel.

— espcially oak — and grazing cattle. Only the occasional rumble of a passing train on the opposite side of the valley disturbs the tranquil atmosphere.

Ahead of you, over a dark hillside of fir trees, stands Restormel Castle, and a steep road leads up to this splendid Norman building. It was one of three guarding Cornwall, the others being at Launceston and Trematon. What we see are the remains of the central keep: the whole castle must have been enormous as even this keep has a circumference of 100 yards.

Back down to the road, our walk continues along the valleyside, beneath Duchy of Cornwall fir plantations. The distant view of Lostwithiel parish church, dedicated to St Bartholomew, reminds me of approaching a town in Brittany as the spire has what I call 'wind vents' in it. A 'broached' spire is, I believe, the correct term.

Lostwithiel is worth a longer visit with its lovely 15th-century bridge, river walks and peaceful atmosphere. It has managed to preserve the feeling that it was once a very important town and port in the 12th century.

And so to the station and home by train. We once did part of this walk with all our six grandchildren in very wet weather in wintertime with the River Fowey in flood. The children loved it!

I do hope you have enjoyed this selection of just a few of our favourite walks and that you will find pleasure in trying them out for yourself.

A distant view of the spire of Lostwithiel church.

WALK CORNWALL EVERY MONTH WITH

CORNISH LIFE MAGAZINE

YOUR COUNTY MAGAZINE

CORNISH LIFE SUBSCRIPTION FORM

Please send a 12 month subscription of *Cornish Life*
(UK £14.00, Overseas £17.00 sterling) to:

Name _____

Address _____

_____

_____ Telephone_____

Commencing with the _____issue

☐ Renewal   ☐ New Subscription (*please tick*)

Your name and address (*if different*)

Name _____

Address _____

_____ Telephone _____

For any further details, or for information on overseas subscriptions contact:

CORNISH LIFE, FINANCE HOUSE, BARNFIELD ROAD, EXETER, DEVON EX1 1QR. Telephone (0392) 216766

WALKING CORNWALL WITH DONALD VAGE BOOK TWO

Ten more favourite walks with Donald and Desirée Vage —
not forgetting their dog Tessa. This second volume includes
walks along the banks of two rivers, across clifftops on the
Lizard, and a fifty mile marathon walk (divided into seven easy
stages) across the spine of Cornwall from Padstow to Fowey
— The Saints' Way.

Exploring the deep winding lanes of Cornwall, the quiet creeks, peaceful moorland heights, wooded river banks, tors and waterfalls, hamlets, villages and churches of his native county has long been a favourite pastime of Truro jeweller Donald Vage. His popular broadcasts on BBC Radio Cornwall and monthly features in *Cornish Life Magazine* have already tempted many people to explore some of the lesser-known areas of their county. Now, Donald Vage has gathered together ten of his favourite coastal and countryside walks in Cornwall — illustrated with maps and photographs — many of which are as well suited to the elderly or disabled as the young and active.